HARTLEPOOL
WITHDRAWN
LIBRARIES

HC

D0295754

1623333 6

ROSEMARY
SHRAGER'S
YORKSHIRE
BREAKFASTS

Photography by Sue Hiscoe

Edited by Sarah Freeman

GREAT NORTHERN

This food is dedicated to anytime of day.

Great Northern Books
PO Box 213, Ilkley, LS29 9WS
www.greatnorthernbooks.co.uk

© Rosemary Shrager 2011

All rights reserved. No part of this book may be reproduced in any form or by any means without permission in writing from the publisher, except by a reviewer who may quote brief passages in a review.

ISBN: 978 1 905080 96 0

Home Economist and Stylist: Gilly Robinson

Photography by Sue Hiscoe

Edited by Sarah Freeman

Design by David Burrill

CIP Data
A catalogue for this book is available
from the British Library

Previous titles by Rosemary Shrager:

ROSEMARY: CASTLE COOK

ROSEMARY SHRAGER'S SCHOOL FOR COOKS

ABSOLUTELY FOOLPROOF CLASSIC HOME
COOKING

CONTENTS

INTRODUCTION

I can honestly say, from the bottom of my heart, that I simply love cooking breakfast. It has to be my favourite meal of the day, especially at weekends when it's possible to spend some leisurely time relaxing over the breakfast table.

Breakfasts have changed considerably in the last 150 years. Back in 1861, Isabella Beeton suggested the country's more well-off households should have a buffet of cold meats from the larder for the first meal of the day, nicely garnished of course. Collared and potted meats or fish, cold game or poultry, veal and ham pies, game and rump steak were all possible on the mid 19th century well-to-do breakfast menu. Isabella also added the following suggestions for hot dishes, "braised fish such as mackerel, whiting, herring, dried haddocks etc, mutton chops and rump steaks, broiled sheep's kidneys, sausages, rashers of bacon, bacon and poached eggs, ham and poached eggs, omelette, plain boiled eggs, oeufs-au-plat, poached eggs on toast, muffins, toast and marmalade and butter."

Reading her list today, the broiled sheep's kidneys aside, much of it sounds quite modern. What has changed is the sheer amount of choice and the copious quantity. Today people take less time over breakfast, it's whatever their taste buds are in need of and most are very specific about what they enjoy first thing in the morning. Some will always start the day with a boiled egg, for others it just has to be a bowl of muesli, but it really doesn't take a lot of time to cook up something interesting. I read recently in a very old book by Lady Jekyll a breakfast that would be perfect for children. She says in *Kitchen Essays*, published in 1921, "Try bananas skinned and halved across, and again lengthwise, and served frizzling from a buttered sauté pan on fried toast, with perhaps a dash of orange juice added, an excellent and wholesome food for the young."

What I have tried to do in this book is cater for everybody's needs. It includes alternatives to the traditional full English, there's a section on simple healthy dishes and a few recipes of sheer indulgence. In Yorkshire, the largest county in Great Britain, we are blessed with an abundance of great producers and fantastic ingredients. No matter where you are, from the coast to the county's largest towns and cities, you will find wonderful people who dedicate their lives to producing the best products. I very rarely have to go outside the county for ingredients and I have tried to make the most of what we have on our doorstep, although I confess, a few more exotic dishes have been included along the way.

The recipes are simple; you cannot go complicated first thing in the morning. The only food that needs a little more thought is the bread, but much of the preparation can be done in advance. It really is worth trying to make your own bread because the taste and the smell is just wonderful.

I know for many, time is in short supply, but making your own preserves can be quite therapeutic. Homemade marmalade is definitely one of my weaknesses and I like taking a jar as a present when visiting friends.

A cooked breakfast is certainly not fashionable to eat every day, but I think it is certainly justifiable to eat a couple of days a week, if not more. You do not have to have a full-blown number; just something simple like grilled kippers, trout or boiled eggs. It really does set you up for the day.

Most of the recipes in this book don't have to just be eaten at breakfast time, dishes such as omelette and herring roe are great for supper. You know what they say, eat breakfast as a king, lunch as a prince and dinner as a pauper.

If you are suffering from the night before, and you end up dehydrated with low blood sugar levels the thing to do is to have a full English breakfast, plus plenty of water and orange juice. They say this does wonders. What a great excuse!

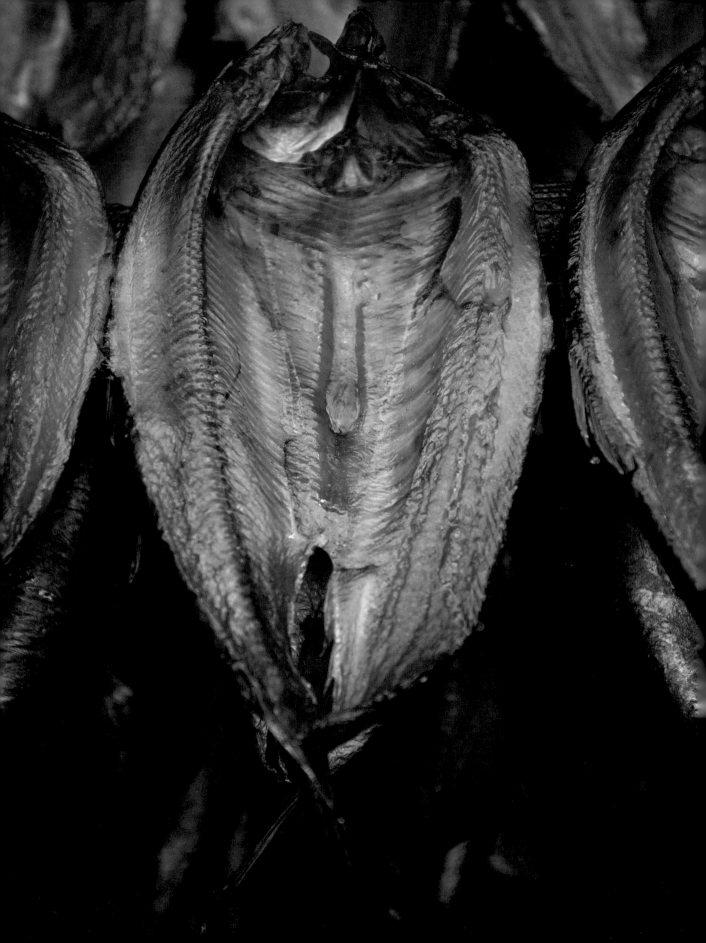

CHAPTER 1

FULL ENGLISH

A full English breakfast is a great opportunity to try local produce. One of my pet hates is the water and salt residue that so often pours out of bacon. However, meat from good quality producers avoids the problem and while Yorkshire is blessed with an abundance of great producers, every area has their own gems, it's just a question of seeking them out. A cooked breakfast with bacon, sausages and all the trimmings is a treat, but remember you do have a whole day to burn off those extra calories. If you fancy a change from the usual bacon, egg and sausage, I've included here a selection of alternative breakfast recipes from sweet potato and corn fritters to brown shrimp omelette.

Nothing takes long to make and really all the perfect breakfast needs is a little organisation. The golden rule is cook everything in advance except the eggs!

FULL ENGLISH BREAKFAST

You can grill your bacon, but I think frying is much more tasty because you get all those lovely flavours in the pan. I know some people are a little nervous of black pudding, but there's really no need. It's made from onion, oatmeal, suet and yes, animal blood. In the Hebrides they use lamb's blood, in Yorkshire they use pig's, but the mixture is boiled for a couple of hours, so all the ingredients are properly cooked through and it really is delicious. I haven't included a recipe for black pudding, but it's always good to know what is in it.

Serves 2

Olive oil
4 pieces of back dry cured bacon
2 pork sausages
2 medium tomatoes
Pinch of sugar
Salt and pepper
1 tsp thyme
10 button mushrooms
2 slices black pudding, approx 1cm thick
2 pieces white bread
2 large eggs

Drizzle a little olive oil into a large frying pan and cook the bacon and the pork sausages on a medium to high heat for 2 minutes on each side. Remove the bacon and put into a dish to keep warm. The pork sausages will need an extra 5 or 6 minutes, turning regularly to ensure an even colour. Once cooked, remove from the frying pan and add to the bacon to keep warm.

Cut the tomatoes in half, horizontal to the stalk and season with sugar, salt, pepper and thyme. Place the open part of the tomato down into the frying pan and fry on a medium to high heat until slightly caramelised. This will take about 3 minutes. Turn the tomato over and cook for a further 3 minutes. Remove and put into a dish to keep warm.

Drizzle a little more oil in the pan. Remove the stalks from the mushrooms and fry for 3 to 4 minutes. Drain in a colander to remove the juices, season and then place in a dish to keep warm.

Put the black pudding into the same frying pan and cook on a medium heat for 2 minutes on each side before placing into the dish with the bacon to keep warm.

Wipe the pan out with some kitchen roll. Place on a medium heat and add a drizzle of olive oil. Remove the crusts from the bread and cut in half. Place into the heated pan and fry until golden brown on both sides. Put in a dish to keep warm.

Wipe the pan out again and drizzle in some more olive oil. Crack in the eggs and cook gently for 5 minutes. For the best result, don't have your heat too high.

If you would like, add the recipe for homemade baked beans on page 25. If not, simply serve and enjoy. What a treat.

SWEET POTATO AND CORN FRITTERS WITH FRIED EGG

This is a quick alternative to fried potatoes and good for vegetarians. The trick is to make sure you season well.

Serves 2

50g flour
1 large egg
130g sweet potato, coarsely grated
130g sweetcorn
1 garlic clove, finely grated
½ tsp chilli
Big pinch of five spice
8 spring onions, finely chopped
Salt and pepper
Sunflower oil for frying
4 large eggs

In a large bowl add the flour and egg. Mix to a thick paste, then add all other ingredients and mix well.

In a non-stick frying pan add a little oil. On a low heat put 4 spoons of the mixture into the pan, flattening each down slightly. Allow to cook for 2-3 minutes. Turn over and cook on the other side. Remove from the heat and keep warm.

Crack the eggs into a large frying pan and cook on a medium heat for 2 to 3 minutes. To serve allow 2 fritters per person, each with a fried egg on top.

FIELD MUSHROOMS ON TOAST

Can you imagine going outside picking mushrooms and taking them back for breakfast? When I was eight-years-old, a horse from a nearby stable would often find its way into our garden. The result in the autumn was wonderful patches of field mushrooms and it was an early lesson in how the natural world works. Field mushrooms are wonderful stuffed and baked in the oven, but this is a really simple recipe which is perfect for breakfast.

Serves 2

2 large field mushrooms
60g butter
2 tbsp water
2 tbsp whipping cream
Salt and pepper
2 slices wholemeal bread
Butter for spreading
2 tbsp curly parsley, finely chopped

First peel the mushrooms by taking a knife and pulling the skin from the side into the centre to reveal clean white flesh. Now cut into slices. Heat the butter in a non-stick frying pan and cook the mushrooms until soft. Add the water and whipping cream. Season well and cook for a further minute. Toast the bread (for wholemeal loaf recipe see page 110) and butter well. Put the mushrooms on top and sprinkle with parsley.

BROWN SHRIMP OMELETTE

Omelettes are such quick and easy breakfasts to make. I've included two different versions here, but the alternatives are endless.

Serves 1

2 large or 3 medium eggs
60g butter
100g brown shrimps
1 tbsp of parsley, finely chopped
Salt and pepper

First peel the shrimps, then heat in a pan with half the butter, parsley, salt and pepper. In a bowl whisk the eggs and season well. Melt the rest of the butter in a small frying pan and pour in the whisked eggs. Leave for a few seconds, then while still undercooked mix around carefully with a fork. Now add the brown shrimps, sprinkling evenly across the omelette. Allow to sit for 30 seconds until the underneath of the omelette is a pale golden colour. Carefully fold the omelette over, slide onto a plate and serve.

YORKSHIRE HAM AND REAL YORKSHIRE WENSLEYDALE OMELETTE

Serves 1

2 large or 3 medium eggs

30g butter

100g slice of ham, diced

40g Real Yorkshire Wensleydale Cheese, very finely grated

Salt and pepper

In a bowl whisk the eggs and season well. Melt the butter in a small frying pan on a medium heat and pour in the whisked eggs. Leave for a few seconds, then while still undercooked mix around carefully with a fork. Now add the diced ham and very finely grated Wensleydale cheese, sprinkling evenly across the omelette. Allow to sit for 30 seconds until the underneath of the omelette is a pale golden colour. Carefully fold the omelette over, slide onto a plate and serve.

BABY TOMATOES ON TOAST WITH SWEET CURED BACON

I adore bacon and tomatoes. The salt in the bacon brings out the flavour of the tomatoes, it's a combination made in heaven.

Serves 2

Olive oil
12 cherry tomatoes, halved
1 tbsp thyme leaves
1 tbsp caster sugar
Salt and pepper
4 pieces sweet cured bacon
2 slices wholemeal bread
Butter for spreading

In a large non-stick frying pan drizzle in some olive oil and place on a medium heat. Lay the baby tomatoes flat side down, if you prefer you can cook them whole, and cook until slightly caramelised. Turn over and sprinkle on thyme leaves, sugar and season with salt and pepper. Turn down the heat and gently move the tomatoes around in the pan for about 5 minutes.

Put the bacon under the grill and cook for 1 minute. Turn over and cook on the other side until crispy being careful not to burn.

Toast the bread and butter it well. Put the toast onto a plate, top with the tomatoes and 2 pieces of bacon.

HOMEMADE BAKED BEANS WITH CRISPY BACON AND SAUTÉED POTATOES

Baked beans are so much nicer made yourself and far more nutritious. I remember making them as a child with bacon and garlic, but they are just as good on their own and I still love the flavour. This recipe makes a large quantity of beans, far more than you will need for the actual dish. However, because of the length of time it takes to prepare, it makes sense to put half in the freezer for next time.

Serves 4

250g dried haricot beans
1 carrot, cut into chunks
1 onion, cut into quarters
1 celery stick, cut into chunks
1 bay leaf
Sprigs of parsley

For the Sautéed Potatoes

4 medium potatoes, peeled
(leftovers work just as well)
Sunflower oil
Salt and pepper
8 slices smoked streaky bacon,
each cut in half.

For the Sauce

Olive oil
300g onions, finely chopped
4 garlic cloves, finely chopped
4 tbsp tomato ketchup
2 tbsp tomato purée
250g tinned chopped tomatoes
2 tbsp sugar
4 drops Tabasco sauce
1 tbsp Henderson's Relish or Worcestershire sauce
400ml bean water

First put the beans in a large saucepan covered in cold water. Add the carrot, onion, celery, bay leaf and parsley. Mix, bring to the boil and then turn down the heat and simmer for 1½ hours. You may need to add more water during cooking if the liquid reduces too much. Once cooked, strain and reserve 400ml of the bean water.

Meanwhile take a large non-stick frying pan and drizzle in some olive oil. Add the onions and garlic and cook for 2 minutes on a low heat. Now add the tomato ketchup, purée, chopped tomato, sugar, Tabasco, Henderson's Relish and the bean water. Cook gently for a further 10 minutes. Remove and blend until smooth. In a large saucepan add the cooked beans and tomato mixture together with a pinch of salt.

Cover and place in the oven at 180°C for 30 minutes, turning down to 150°C for a further 1¼ to 1 ½ hours. Remove and store until required.

Boil the potatoes until just cooked, drain well and allow to get cold. When ready to have your meal, drizzle some oil in a large frying pan on a medium to high heat. Cut the potatoes into slices approx 5mm in thickness. Put into the frying pan and cook until golden brown on one side. Turn over and cook on the other side. Remove from the heat, season and keep warm until ready to serve.

Finally in a medium saucepan add the chopped bacon and cook until crispy. Discard any excess fat, pour in some of the beans and heat through. Serve with the sautéed potatoes.

SMOKED BACON WITH SPICY TOMATO SAUCE AND SODA BREAD

Serves 4

8 rashers of smoky bacon
4 slices soda bread, toasted

For the Spicy Tomato Sauce
500g tomatoes, quartered
2 red chillies
4 cloves of garlic
2 tbsp hoisin sauce
2 tbsp Henderson's relish or Worcestershire sauce
1 rounded tbsp sugar
1 tbsp white wine vinegar
1 tsp English dried mustard
1 tbsp olive oil
Salt and pepper

Place all the tomato sauce ingredients into a processor and blend until smooth. Pour into a non-stick sauce pan and on a medium heat bring to the boil. Turn down the heat to low and reduce the liquid to a thick sauce. This can take up to an hour, and be careful not to burn the bottom of the pan by stirring frequently.

Now fry the bacon. I like mine crispy, but it works just as well however you like it. Place onto the toasted soda bread (for soda bread recipe see page 111) with a dollop of sauce. The rest of the sauce will keep in the fridge and is great with pasta, baked potatoes or even as a salad dressing.

KEDGEREE

This reminds me of my grandmother. She loved making kedgeree and her secret was to use plenty of chopped parsley.

Serves 4

250g smoked haddock
400ml milk
200g basmati rice
100g butter
1 small onion, peeled and chopped
2 tsp curry powder
4 eggs, hard boiled, shelled and cut into quarters
3 tbsp parsley, chopped
Salt and black pepper
Water to cover

Place the smoked haddock in a frying pan and add the milk. Cover the pan and cook over a low heat until the fish flakes easily. You will need to watch closely to prevent the milk from boiling over. Strain the haddock, remove the skin and then flake the fish.

Rinse the rice in cold water and then put into a saucepan. Pour in salted water to ½ cm above the rice. Cover, bring to the boil and reduce to a simmer for approx 8 minutes without stirring or until the water has been absorbed and the grains are soft. Fork through the rice and set aside.

Melt half the butter in a large saucepan and gently sauté the onion until soft, but not browned. Add the curry powder and cook for 30 seconds. Now add the cooked rice, eggs, smoked haddock and gently fold over with the remaining butter, parsley and seasoning.

FRIED HERRINGS IN OATMEAL

I first ate these on the Isle of Harris. Ever since it's been one of my favourite ways of eating fresh herring and the only thing to remember is not to have the heat too high.

Serves 4

150g medium oatmeal
Salt and pepper
4 whole herrings (ask your fishmonger to remove the bones)
60g butter
Olive oil
1 lemon, cut into wedges

Put the oatmeal, seasoned with salt and pepper, into a large gratin dish. Take each fish and cover with the oatmeal, pressing it onto the fish. In a large frying pan, melt half the butter with a drizzle of oil. Place 2 herrings into the pan and cook on a low heat for approx 2 minutes on each side. Put on a plate and keep warm. Repeat with the final 2 herrings. Serve with the wedges of lemon and wholemeal bread (for wholemeal bread recipe see page 110).

GRILLED WHITBY KIPPERS

One of the traditional ways of cooking kippers is jugging. Simply place the kippers in a tall jug, heads down - tails can be left out - pour over boiling water, cover and after 5 minutes they will be ready to be served with butter. Alternatively, you can cook them in a frying pan on a gentle heat or bake in the oven with plenty of butter over the top. I prefer to grill them, but whichever method you use, always try to buy natural smoked kippers as you really can't beat the taste.

Serves 2

2 kippers
60g butter, melted

Put the kippers skin side down onto a baking tray. Pour the melted butter all over the kippers and place under a medium grill. Cook for 4 minutes or until just starting to brown. Serve with wholemeal toast (for wholemeal loaf recipe see page 110).

CHAPTER 2

HEALTHY BREAKFASTS

One of the most important things is never to leave the house on an empty stomach. After going overnight without food, energy reserves will be low and if you are trying to lose weight there's a temptation to skip breakfast. This often backfires. By mid-morning you're often so hungry that you grab anything you can get your hands on regardless of the calories.

So the trick is to start the day with a good healthy breakfast, something simple like smoked haddock with poached eggs or a bowl of porridge. I have also included here some recipes for making your own yoghurt and homemade muesli, which will definitely set you up for the day and will certainly stop you from snacking.

MUESLI

Muesli is all about a question of taste. Some people don't like dried fruit, some people don't like sugar and I have to confess I'm also a little fussy. In summer when I have fresh fruit with my muesli, I do not like any dried fruit in the mix, but in winter I find the dried fruit gives it a real lift. Here, are four different combinations that I love, but feel free to experiment.

MUESLI WITHOUT DRIED FRUIT, SUGAR FREE

Serves 4 to 8

200g rolled oats
25g sesame seeds
25g flaked almonds
30g sunflower seeds
25g pumpkin seeds
10g golden linseed
15g walnuts, chopped
25g Brazil nuts, roughly chopped
10g or 2 level tbsp wheat bran

Mix everything together and put into an airtight container.

MUESLI WITH DRIED FRUIT

Serves 4 to 8

200g rolled oats
25g pumpkin seeds
30g Brazil nuts, roughly chopped
25g flaked almonds
30g seedless raisins
30g Medjool dates, chopped
20g dried apricot, chopped
10g or 2 tbsp wheat bran
1 tbsp soft brown sugar

Mix everything together and put into an airtight container.

MUESLI WITH EXOTIC DRIED FRUIT AND NUTS

Serves 4 to 8

200g rolled oats
40g flaked almonds
40g sunflower seeds
30g Brazil nuts, roughly chopped
20g dried pineapple, chopped
20g crystallised ginger, chopped
10g dried mango, chopped
20g Medjool dates, chopped
10g or 2 tbsp wheat bran

Mix everything together and put into an airtight container.

MUESLI WITH FIGS, CRANBERRIES AND CINNAMON

Serves 4 to 8

200g rolled oats
40g dried figs, chopped
20g dried cranberries
30g sunflower seeds
20g flaked almonds
15g sesame seeds
25g Brazil nuts, roughly chopped
1 tsp cinnamon
15g unrefined golden caster sugar
10g or 2 tbsp wheat bran

Mix everything together and put into an airtight container.

HEALTHY PORRIDGE

My personal trainer Katie tells me she eats porridge nearly every morning with strawberry jam and if it's good enough for her, it's good enough for me. There are a few ways of cooking porridge. Some use full fat milk, some don't; some like it runny, others prefer it thick. I tend to use water with plenty of salt. If you don't want to use the salt, then do use milk or the porridge will taste a little bland. Once you have cooked the recipe below, you can adapt it any way you like until you find a version which suits your particular taste.

Serves 1 large portion.

50g porridge oats
300ml water or milk or mixed
1 tsp salt

Optional ideas for topping:
2 tbsp honey
Brown sugar
Greek yoghurt
Blueberries
Bran
Bananas

Put the oats, water and salt into a small saucepan and bring to a simmer, slowly stirring all the time. Keep simmering for 6–8 minutes until thick. Pour into serving bowl and if you desire add fresh fruit, yoghurt and honey.

YOGHURT

Most people don't make their own yoghurt, but it is so simple and so much cheaper than the shop bought variety. The only thing you need to watch is that the temperature is warm and constant and it may be useful to have a thermometer. You can use a yoghurt maker to incubate the yoghurt or a wide-mouthed thermos flask. If you don't have either, you can achieve the same result by putting your container in an airing cupboard or, if you are lucky enough to have one, an Aga.

1 litre full fat milk
1 tbsp plain live yoghurt, fresh

In a heavy bottomed saucepan, heat the milk to a simmer, around 76-82°C. Keep at this heat for at least 2 minutes, stirring constantly and ensuring the milk does not overheat.

When finished, remove the pan from the heat and allow to cool enough to be able to put your finger in the mixture (if you are using a thermometer, the temperature should be between 40°C and 45°C). Mix the tablespoon of live yoghurt to loosen. Add to the pot of warmed milk and stir until it has dissolved.

Place in a wide brimmed flask or container, cover, and maintain a constant warm temperature until it thickens. This will take 6 to 8 hours. Avoid disturbing during this time or the yoghurt may not set. You can test to see if it is ready by gently turning the container. If it keeps its shape, it's done. Cover and refrigerate. Yoghurt will keep in the fridge for 6-7 days. A yellow liquid may appear on top of the yoghurt. This is whey and you can either pour it off or just mix it into the yoghurt when you eat it.

SMOKED HADDOCK WITH POACHED EGG

This is such a healthy breakfast, one I often have when I stay in hotels if I want something lighter than the usual full English.

Serves 2

2 fillets smoked haddock
40g butter
Milk, to cover
2 eggs
Salt and pepper
Fresh parsley to garnish

Put the 2 fillets in a pan with the butter and just enough milk to cover. Bring to a simmer and cook for 2 to 3 minutes. Turn the heat off and allow to stand for 5 minutes.

To poach the egg see page 45. Carefully remove the fillet from the milk, drain, season and put onto a plate with the poached egg on top. Garnish with a little parsley.

ORANGE AND GRAPEFRUIT SALAD

My mother-in-law, Irene Shrager, always made this fruit salad. It's one I have enjoyed many times and again its beauty is in its simplicity.

Serves 2

3 oranges
1 pink grapefruit
Fresh mint to garnish

Remove the outer peel and pith of the grapefruit and oranges by cutting down to the flesh with a sharp knife. Then go in between the sections and cut out the segments, making sure not to leave on any pith or skin. Put the prepared fruit into a bowl and squeeze the remaining juice from the core and skin over it. Place in a bowl and serve with some fresh mint.

SUMMER FRUIT SALAD

I have chosen my favourite fruit, but you can choose any combination you like. You can have a three melon fruit salad, a fig fruit salad, it's endless, but that's really the fun of it.

Serves 6

2 peaches
1 punnet strawberries
1 punnet redcurrants
Bunch of green grapes
1 punnet raspberries
Juice of 2 oranges
Fresh mint, chopped
Sprinkle of caster sugar
(optional)

Dice the peaches into small chunks and put into a bowl. Wash, de hull and finely dice the strawberries and add to the bowl. Destalk the redcurrants, cut the green grapes in half and add both to the bowl along with the raspberries. Now add the juice of the oranges, chopped fresh mint and caster sugar if desired. Serve with yoghurt (for yoghurt recipe see page 41).

WINTER STEWED FRUIT

Dried fruits are high in fibre and important minerals, including iron, which is good for skin, hair and nails. However, they also contain quite a lot of natural sugar so you shouldn't add too much. In this case a little goes a long way.

Serves 4

250g prunes, pitted and soaked overnight
250g dried apricots
150g figs (optional)
1 orange
Water, to cover
1 vanilla pod cut in half lengthways
100g caster sugar or honey

Put the prunes, apricots and, if using, the figs into a medium saucepan. Cut strips of peel from the orange. Leaving the pith, squeeze and strain the juice. Add the peel and the juice to the fruit and cover with water. Add the vanilla pod and the sugar and simmer for 10 minutes. Remove and allow to cool for 4 hours or ideally overnight.

- At Christmas you can use cinnamon sticks, cloves, ginger or anything that takes your fancy.

CHAPTER 3

BRUNCH

Brunch is a meal when you have the full works. The difference between a large breakfast and brunch is the time you eat, brunch starts around 10.30am to 11am and finishes around 12pm to 12.30pm. It is a wonderful weekend alternative to breakfast and lunch and it gives you the whole afternoon to go out on a long walk or drive to the coast.

One of the best brunches I ever had was in New York when my sister-in-law Anne was living there. With the American side of the family and a group of friends we had smoked salmon, bacon bagels, fruit, muesli, toast, eggs, bread and copious amounts of coffee and fresh orange juice. The meal took hours to eat, but it was so much fun and brunch is always a great way to entertain family and friends.

BAKED EGG EN COCOTTE

This is probably one of the simplest recipes in the book, but the fun is experimenting with different flavours from chorizo and parsley to cheese, ham, mushroom and even mussels.

Serves 4
4 120g ramekins
4 dstsp butter
4 large fresh eggs
4 tbsp double cream
Salt and white pepper

First grease the ramekins with half the butter and sprinkle on a little salt. Carefully crack one egg into each ramekin. Season the double cream with salt and white pepper. Melt the rest of the butter, add to the cream and pour the mixture over the eggs. Carefully place the ramekins into a gratin dish filled halfway with water. Bake in the oven at 180°C for 15 minutes or until the eggs are just set.

BAKED EGG WITH HAM AND MUSHROOM

Serves 4

4 120g ramekins
60g butter
100g mushroom, finely chopped
2 tbsp parsley, finely chopped
Salt and pepper
125g ham, finely diced
4 large eggs
4 tbsp double cream
Salt and white pepper

First grease the ramekins with half the butter and sprinkle on a little salt. Melt the rest of the butter in a large frying pan. Cook the mushrooms for 5 minutes, then add the parsley, salt, pepper and finally the ham. Place a spoonful of the mixture into the bottom of each buttered ramekin, then carefully crack in one egg. Season the double cream with salt and white pepper and pour the mixture over the eggs. Carefully place the ramekins into a gratin dish filled halfway with water. Bake in the oven at 180°C for 15 minutes or until the eggs are just set.

BUBBLE AND SQUEAK CAKES WITH ROASTED BABY TOMATOES

I was brought up on bubble and squeak, which is really just leftover potatoes and sprouts. It was a very popular supper dish in our house and is always great for breakfast. If you like, you can make this recipe as one big cake and serve in the pan.

Serves 2

300g potatoes, peeled
150g medium-sized
Brussel sprouts
1 bunch spring onions,
finely chopped
Salt and pepper
50g butter
10 baby vine tomatoes
Extra virgin olive oil
Salt and pepper
Pinch of sugar

If you haven't got any leftover vegetables, first boil the potatoes until soft, drain well and mash. Remove the outer leaves from the sprouts and boil for 4 minutes until cooked. Drain and refresh under cold water. Finely chop the sprouts and add to the mashed potato with the spring onions. Season well with salt and pepper.

Fill 5cm rings or squares with the mixture to about 1.5cm in depth. Pat down, remove the ring and repeat until all the potato mixture is finished. If possible put into the fridge for an hour to help the mixture set.

Melt the butter on a medium heat in a non-stick frying pan. Place a few cakes in the pan and cook for 3 minutes or so until the bottom is golden brown. Turn over with 2 spatulas (it's easier to manage) and cook on the other side for another 3 minutes or until golden brown. Remove and keep warm.

Put the tomatoes into a greased oven-proof dish, sprinkle with olive oil, over season with salt and pepper and sugar. Put into the oven at 200°C for 15 to 20 minutes and serve with the cakes.

YORKSHIRE GAMMON WITH SPICED PICKLED PEARS

I have made a slightly larger quantity of spiced pears than is strictly necessary because it is a fruit that can stand on its own and looks so pretty on the table.

Serves 4

40g butter
1 tsp olive oil
2 300g gammon slices, each cut into 2 pieces
Salt and pepper

For the spiced pears
4 whole pears
1 vanilla pod
3 star anise
4 whole cloves
1 stick cinnamon
1 orange, peel only
120g caster sugar
Water to cover

In a saucepan large enough to hold 4 pears, put in the vanilla, star anise, cloves, cinnamon, orange peel, sugar and water. Bring to the heat and simmer gently for 5 minutes. Peel the pears, leaving the stalks on, but removing the core from the base. Place into the spiced syrup and cook gently for 20 to 25 minutes until soft. Remove and allow to cool in the syrup. Drain well and serve either standing up or cut in half lengthwise.

In a frying pan add the butter and oil and cook the gammon gently on a medium heat for 2 minutes on each side. Season or keep warm, and serve with half a spiced cooked pear.

SEARED MACKEREL IN BUTTER AND PARSLEY WITH SAUTÉED POTATOES

To me there is nothing better than the smell of fresh mackerel straight from the sea, frying in a pan on a fire on the beach. While it might not be quite as romantic, it's just as tasty done at home.

Serves 2

2 mackerel fillets
Salt and pepper
2 tbsp flour
60g butter
Olive oil
2 tbsp parsley, finely chopped
1 lemon

For sautéed potatoes recipe see page 25

First season the fillets on both sides, but dredge the skin side only in flour. In a non-stick frying pan, melt 20g butter and a drizzle of olive oil on a medium heat. Add the mackerel skin side down and cook for 2 minutes. Turn over and cook on the other side for a further minute, adding the rest of the butter and half the parsley. Baste well to keep the fish moist. Remove and serve on sautéed potatoes with a squeeze of lemon on top.

GRILLED TROUT

This no frills dish may be plain, but it's simply delicious. With Swinton Trout farm just on my doorstep I couldn't not include a recipe for plain grilled trout and while I've allowed one fillet per person, if you're feeling hungry go for two.

Serves 2

1 whole 500g trout, filleted and pin bones removed
Salt and pepper
2 lemons
40g butter, melted (optional)

Put the two trout fillets onto a well greased baking tray, skin side up, and season with salt and pepper. Squeeze over ½ the lemon and pour over the melted butter. Put under a hot grill for 2 minutes. Turn the fillets over and add the rest of the butter and a squeeze of lemon. Put back under the grill for another 2-3 minutes. If you are able, remove the skin from the fillets, then serve with a wedge of lemon on the side.

RIBBLESDALE SUPERIOR GOAT'S CHEESE AND SPINACH OMELETTE

This Ribblesdale Superior Goat's Cheese is as good as any French cheese you can find; delicious if you are a goat's cheese lover.

Serves 1

50g spinach
50g butter
Salt and pepper
1 tbsp parsley, finely chopped
2 large or 3 medium eggs
50g Ribblesdale Superior goat's cheese, crumbled

First wilt the spinach in a small frying pan with 20g butter, season well and fold in the parsley. Now drain and gently squeeze out the excess water.

In a bowl, whisk the eggs and season well. Take the same small frying pan and melt the rest of the butter on a medium heat. Pour in the whisked eggs, leave for a few seconds, then while still undercooked mix around carefully with a fork. Keep stirring with the fork, and while still slightly runny in the middle add the crumbled goat's cheese, spinach and parsley. Leave for 30 seconds, then fold in half and leave for another 30 seconds. Slide onto a plate and serve.

HOT SMOKED TROUT WITH CREAMY SCRAMBLED EGGS AND DILL ON A MUFFIN

The most important part of this recipe is the scrambled eggs which must be slightly undercooked and creamy. The wonderful thing is that once you've bought the hot smoked trout, it keeps in the fridge for a reasonable length of time and it is so useful if you have people coming to stay for the weekend.

Serves 4

8 large eggs
Salt and pepper
4 tbsp double cream (optional)
30g butter
2 muffins, halved (for muffin recipe see page 117)
2 fillets of hot smoked trout
1 tbsp dill, chopped
1 tbsp chives, chopped
Butter for spreading

First put the eggs into a bowl with salt and pepper and whisk well. If using, add the double cream and mix. In a non-stick pan, melt the butter on a low heat. Now add the eggs, stirring all the time. Toast the muffins and spread with butter. While the eggs are still not quite cooked flake in the trout. Gently fold into the eggs, trying to keep the flakes intact. Serve on the muffin and sprinkle with chives and dill.

CRAB FISH CAKES

These crab cakes are great to freeze. I like to use fresh crab meat and if possible do try to prepare the crabs yourself. Obviously this is too much to do at breakfast, which is why it's good to make a batch in advance.

Serves 4

300g potato (weight after peeling)
300g fresh white crab meat
100g fresh brown crab meat
1 egg-yolk
2 tbsp coriander, chopped
Zest of 1 lime
½ red birds' eye chilli, finely chopped
Salt and pepper
Plain flour, to dust
3 eggs
100g fine white breadcrumbs
90g butter
Sunflower oil for frying

Boil the potatoes until soft, drain well and mash. Put into a large bowl with the crab, egg yolk, coriander, lime zest, chilli, salt and pepper. Using your hands, shape into 8 patties then dip into flour and allow to get cold and firm. Assemble two bowls, the first containing the beaten eggs, the second containing the breadcrumbs. Dip the patties in each bowl in that order and fry gently in the oil and butter for 3 minutes on each side.

PORK SAUSAGES WITH CARAMELISED ONION

Sausages are one of the products that until you are shown how easy they are to make you wouldn't even dream of trying. You can buy sausage-making attachments for food mixers or you can buy a free standing one. I really think that it is great investment because sausages are such fun to make, absolutely delicious and great alternatives to hamburgers.

Serves 4–6

For the caramelised onion

2 tbsp olive oil

30g butter

4 red onions, peeled and finely sliced

40g caster sugar

Salt and pepper

For the sausages

800g belly of pork, finely minced

50g fresh breadcrumbs

25g parsley, finely chopped, optional

3 tsp thyme

3 tsp pepper

2 tsp salt or to taste

Sausage skins

25g lard

To make the caramelised red onion, put the oil and butter into a large frying pan. Add the onions and cook on a low heat for 30 minutes. Turn the heat up a little and add the sugar. Cook for a further 5 to 10 minutes. Season well, allow to cool, and put into the fridge until required. To serve put into a small pan and gently heat.

To make the sausages, put the minced pork, breadcrumbs, parsley, thyme, pepper and salt into a bowl and mix well. To test they are well seasoned, fry a small patty in a pan with a drizzle of oil. Once cooked, taste and if needed add more salt and pepper to the mixture. Put the sausage meat into the casings. Ideally, this needs to be done with a sausage machine. Allow to rest for at least an hour before frying; overnight would be even better. Melt the lard in a pan and fry the sausages on a medium heat until browned all over. They can be roasted in the oven or grilled, but there is nothing like a sizzling sausage.

CHAPTER 4

THE MUNCHIES

What can I say about the munchies except that you get them on occasions, day or night. I have given you a selection of recipes that I enjoy at any time. Most are quick and easy – if you cut the potato scones small enough they won't take long at all and the cheesy puffs are very satisfying; the only thing is you cannot make them quickly enough!

EGGY BREAD WITH CINNAMON

Serves 2

3 eggs
Salt and pepper
1 tsp sugar
½ tsp cinnamon
60g butter for frying
2 thick slices of white bread
50ml double cream (optional)

Put the eggs into a large bowl, season with salt and pepper and whisk well. Add the sugar, cinnamon and, if using, the double cream, beat well and pour into a baking dish.

Place the bread into the egg mixture and leave for 1 minute. Turn the bread over and leave for 2 minutes to soak. Melt half the butter in a large frying pan on a medium heat. Cook the bread on both sides until golden brown, remove, and repeat with the second slice of bread. To serve, you can sprinkle a little sugar on top.

POTATO SCONES

This mixture is a little bit like gnocchi, but it has to be handled quite gently. When the scones are cooked they firm up considerably, so don't be tempted to add more flour early on. The trick is to cook the scones on a moderate to low heat and, for me, the nicest way to eat them is simply spread with butter or with a poached egg.

Serves 4

300g potatoes,
peeled and cut into
chunks
20g very soft butter
½ tsp salt
90g plain flour
Extra flour for dusting

Cook the potatoes in boiling, salted water until tender, then drain thoroughly. Leave in the colander for a few minutes to steam off excess moisture. Mash the potatoes until smooth (or push them through a potato ricer or sieve) and then allow to get cold. Now add the soft butter and salt. Sieve over the flour, working it in until the dough is smooth; you may need to add a little more flour if the mixture is too sticky.

Turn the dough out onto a well-floured work surface and gently roll out into a 25cm square, about 5mm thick. Cut into 8 rectangles. If you have time, put them in the fridge for one hour, but you can cook them straight away if necessary.

Heat a dry, heavy-based frying pan or a flat griddle over a moderate heat. Test to see if it is hot enough by dusting with a little flour – when it turns golden, the pan is ready. Add the potato scones and cook over a fairly low heat for 5–10 minutes, turning once, until browned on both sides and cooked through. Serve immediately.

FRITTATA

This is quick to make, tasty — you can use any herbs you like - and really useful if you have a few people for breakfast.

Serves 4

4 tbsp olive oil
500g waxy potatoes, peeled and cut into 2 cm cubes
1 onion, chopped
6 medium eggs
Salt and pepper
Handful of chives, parsley, tarragon, all finely chopped
Extra parsley, finely chopped

In a large non-stick frying pan add 3 tbsp of the olive oil. Gently cook the potatoes without browning. This can take up to 20 minutes on a low heat and once cooked put on a plate. In the same pan add the remaining oil and the onion. Soften for 5 minutes, again without letting the onion brown. Remove and add to the potatoes.

Wipe out the pan and on a low heat drizzle in a little olive oil. Put the eggs into a bowl and whisk and season well. Add the chopped herbs, onion and potato. Season again. Pour into the frying pan and cook on a low heat for about 5 minutes, before placing under a grill for a further 5 minutes. Remove, turn over onto a plate and then put back into the frying pan on a low heat for another 3 minutes. Serve sprinkled with parsley.

FOUNTAINS GOLD RAREBIT

I like to make the rarebit in advance, even the day before. If you fancy having it for supper you can substitute the milk for Old Peculier beer, but remember while it's quite delicious, it's also very rich. This recipe makes far more than you need, but the remaining mixture can be kept in the fridge for three to four days.

Serves 4

30g butter
30g flour
100ml milk
200g Fountains Gold cheese, grated
1 tsp Worcestershire sauce
½ tsp English mustard
4 drops Tabasco
Salt and pepper
2 egg yolks
4 slices of bread

First melt the butter in a medium saucepan and add the flour to make a roux. Then add the milk and whisk until it starts to thicken. Add the cheese, Worcester sauce, mustard, Tabasco, salt and pepper and mix well. Allow to cool for 10 minutes. Add the egg yolks and mix again. Make the toast and put a dollop of the mixture on each piece. Place under the grill until golden brown.

REAL YORKSHIRE WENSLEYDALE CHEESY PUFFS

I started making these when the children were young, they loved them and I still do. Made with Real Yorkshire Wensleydale they work a treat.

250ml water
100g butter
150g plain flour, sifted
5 eggs
100g Real Yorkshire Wensleydale cheese
Pinch of salt and pepper
A little grated nutmeg
Sunflower oil for frying

In a pan, bring the water and the butter to the boil together. Add the sifted flour all at once and beat vigorously until the dough comes away clean from both the dish and the spoon. Remove from the stove and continue to beat the dough for a further minute. Add one whole egg and stir vigorously until it is thoroughly mixed with the dough. Stir in the remaining eggs one by one, in the same way, then the grated cheese, pepper, nutmeg and salt. Keep working the dough, until it is completely smooth.

Heat a deep-fat frying pan of oil to 180°C. Take 2 rounded soup spoons and filling one with dough use the other to shape a ball, then roll into the hot oil. When the puffs are golden brown they are ready. Remove from oil and drain on kitchen paper. Serve hot.

Small puffs may be cooked in a hot oven 220°C. Butter a baking sheet and using a forcing bag (or 2 teaspoons) form pastry puffs to about the size of a walnut.

CHAPTER 5

SPECIAL OCCASION

There are so many special occasions to celebrate from birthdays to anniversaries the list is endless. All are a wonderful excuse to have a special breakfast, which, it goes without saying, must be enjoyed at leisure.

I love the smoked haddock soufflé with poached egg and also the Eggs Benedict, but I really think anything goes because it's the little touches that count, like someone else doing the cooking, laying the table beautifully with a linen cloth, napkins and flowers to give it a special touch, or just taking it in on a tray to have breakfast in bed. This is definitely an excuse to pull out all the stops. So enjoy!

SMOKED SALMON AND CREAM CHEESE WITH SODA SCONES

This is based on the traditional cream cheese and smoked salmon bagel, but a soda scone is a good alternative.

Serves 4

For the soda scones
250g plain flour
1 level tsp salt
1 level tsp bicarbonate of soda
250ml buttermilk

For the topping
150g cream cheese
400g smoked salmon
Black pepper
Fresh chives, chopped
1 lemon

First make the scones by putting the flour into a bowl with the salt and bicarbonate of soda and mix well. Add the buttermilk and carefully and lightly mix the flour into a light dough. Make into a ball and put onto a floured surface. With hands dusted in flour, pat down the dough into a round about 1cm thick. Cut the dough into 4.

Place into a dry non-stick pan and, keeping the dough apart, cook on a low heat for 6 minutes. Turn over and cook on the other side for 6 minutes. Remove and place onto a rack.

While still slightly warm, cut each one in half horizontally. Spread some cream cheese onto each half then put a large slice of smoked salmon on top. Sprinkle with black pepper and chives and serve with a squeeze of lemon.

This dish works just as well with round drop pancakes, (for round drop pancake recipe see page 73).

FRIED YORKSHIRE GAMMON AND THE PERFECT FRIED EGG

One of the many things Yorkshire can be proud of is its gammon. This is a classic dish and it's definitely one of those times when it's all about the product.

Serves 2

30g butter
Olive oil
350g slice of gammon, cut into 2 pieces
2 eggs
Salt and pepper

In a large frying pan melt 10g butter and a drizzle of olive oil on a medium heat. Cook the gammon for 2 minutes on each side. Remove and keep warm while you cook the eggs.

Wipe the pan out and again on a medium heat add the remaining butter and another drizzle of oil. When it starts to sizzle, crack the eggs into the pan. Baste the eggs with butter and oil mixture during cooking. You can flip the eggs over, known as 'over easy', but I like to see mine sunny side up. Season with salt and pepper and serve on the gammon.

CLASSIC CHEDDAR CHEESE SOUFFLÉ

Despite what some people may tell you, soufflés are not that difficult. You must make sure all your bowls are clean before you start, but really it's just practise and having confidence.

1 large soufflé dish or 6 individual ramekins.

50g Parmesan cheese, grated

30g unsalted butter

30g plain flour

250g full fat milk

120g strong Fountains Gold cheese or cheddar, grated

Good pinch of cayenne pepper

Salt and white pepper

4 egg yolks

6 egg whites

Butter for greasing

First grease the inside of the ramekins or soufflé dish, then sprinkle all over with the grated Parmesan cheese.

Melt the butter in a small pan, add the flour, mix well and cook for 1 minute. Now slowly add the milk, whisking all the time to ensure sure there are no lumps. Continue mixing until all the milk has been used. Cook for 2 minutes, then add the Fountains Gold cheese. Mix until completely melted, then add the cayenne pepper and season well with salt and pepper. The seasoning needs to be strong because the egg white will dilute the flavour. Allow to cool to just warm then add the egg yolks and mix well.

Now beat the egg whites with a pinch of salt and whisk to a soft peak. Put the cheesy mixture into a large bowl and whisk in one third of the egg whites to loosen the mixture. Now fold in the rest trying to keep as much air in as possible. Fill the soufflé dish or ramekins. Wipe your thumb around the inside edge to stop it from sticking and smooth the tops with a palette knife. Put into the oven at 190°C for 20 to 25 minutes for the large soufflé. For the small ramekins, place on a tray and cook for 8 minutes.

EGGS FLORENTINE

This is a European dish, but we have local eggs and spinach, so I have included it as it is a real treat for a special occasion. I tend to prepare in two individual eared dishes or you can serve in an oven-proof dish.

Serves 2

150g baby spinach
40g butter
Salt and pepper
Freshly grated nutmeg
2 eggs
2 tbsp hollandaise sauce
(for recipe see page 93)
or double cream
2 tbsp cheddar cheese,
finely grated
Sprinkle of Parmesan
cheese, finely grated
(optional)

Wash the spinach and shake off the excess water. Put it in a large saucepan, cover and cook until it has wilted. Drain thoroughly in a sieve, pushing the spinach with the back of a spoon to get out all the water. Return to the pan with the butter, salt and pepper and a good grating of nutmeg. Heat through while you poach the eggs (for poached egg recipe see page 45)

To serve, divide the spinach between two warm eared dishes. Make a hole in the middle, then put an egg on top, sprinkle with the grated cheddar and, if using, the Parmesan. Place under the grill until pale golden in colour or bake in the oven for 5 minutes until the cheese has melted. Cover with hollandaise sauce and serve immediately.

EGGS BENEDICT

Again this is not a Yorkshire dish, but all the produce is.

Serves 4

8 rashers of smoky bacon or slices of ham

Olive oil for frying

4 eggs

4 English muffins, split in half (for English muffin recipe see page 117)

Parsley, finely chopped to garnish

For the hollandaise sauce

250g unsalted butter

2 tbsp white wine vinegar

2 tbsp water

1 bay leaf

1 tsp white peppercorns

4 medium egg yolks

Juice of 1 lemon, or to taste

Sea salt and white pepper

For the hollandaise sauce, first clarify the butter. Put the butter in a small heavy bottomed pan over a very low heat and leave until it has completely melted and the milky residue has separated. Skim off any froth from the top and pour off the clear butter, leaving the residue behind, which can be discarded. Allow the clarified butter to cool slightly.

Put the vinegar, water, bay leaf and white peppercorns into a small, heavy-based pan. Bring to the boil and when the liquid has reduced to the equivalent of a tablespoon, strain into a bowl and allow to cool slightly.

Set a medium-sized bowl over a pan of simmering water, making sure the water doesn't touch the base of the bowl. Pour the reduction into the bowl and switch off the heat (the gentle heat from the hot water beneath the bowl will be enough to cook the hollandaise).

Lightly whisk the egg yolks and add them to the reduction. Stir until they start to slightly thicken to a cream. Very slowly pour in the clarified butter, whisking constantly with a balloon whisk.

If the mixture becomes too thick, briefly turn the heat back on low, but make sure the hollandaise doesn't overheat – you do not want the sauce to separate after all your hard work (if it does, you can try rescuing it by adding another whisked egg yolk to the mixture).

When all the butter has been added, stir in the lemon juice and season well with salt and white pepper.

If using bacon, fry it in a little olive oil until crisp. Remove and keep warm. Now poach the eggs (for poached egg recipe see page 45). Toast the muffins and place onto 4 warmed serving plates (for English Muffins recipe see page 117). Top each half with a bacon rasher or a slice of ham. Place the poached eggs on top and spoon over the hollandaise. Sprinkle with chopped parsley and serve.

DEVILLED LAMB KIDNEYS ON TOAST

This is a dish which has gone out of fashion, it's a shame because it is delicious. I'm including it here with the hope of starting a renaissance.

Serves 2

4 lambs kidney, 250g approx, skinned and white gristle removed
Flour to dust
Salt and pepper
Big pinch of chilli powder
1 tsp Worcester Sauce
1 level tsp dried mustard
1 tsp tomato purée
1 tbsp hoisin sauce
100ml chicken stock
40g butter

2 slices wholemeal bread (for recipe see page 110)
Butter for spreading

First cut the kidneys lengthways, remove the white gristle then cut each half into two. Season the flour with salt and chilli powder and dust the kidneys making sure to shake off any excess. In a bowl, add the Worcester sauce, powdered mustard, tomato purée and hoisin sauce. Mix well, then add half the chicken stock and mix again.

Melt the butter in a large frying pan on a medium heat and fry the floured kidneys for 2 minutes on each side. Now add the devilled mixture, ensuring the kidneys are evenly coated. Taste for seasoning and then cook for a further minute. If the sauce is a little thick, add the rest of the chicken stock as required. Make the toast, butter well and put the kidneys on top.

CHAPTER 6

INDULGENCE

Everyone indulges at one time or another. I see this as a breakfast at about 11am that will set you up for the rest of the day a little like the brunch. All the dishes are very over-doused with calories, but they are absolutely delicious. While it is not sensible to have these dishes too often, I do feel that once in a blue moon it is okay and the soft herring roe really are the biggest treat.

FRIED SOFT HERRING ROE ON BUTTERY TOAST

This is the most wonderful breakfast or supper dish. It's very rich and contains a lot of calories, but if you know you're going to have a very active day this is a perfect start. It is the ultimate comfort food.

Serves 4

100g flour
Salt and pepper
500g soft herring roe (these are impossible to find in supermarkets, but a good fishmonger should be able to help)
80g butter

4 slices bread
Butter for spreading
1 lemon, cut into wedges

First mix the flour, salt and pepper together and dust the herring roe well in the flour. In a non-stick frying pan heat half the butter and fry half the roes for about 2 minutes on each side until golden brown. Remove and keep warm. Now wipe out the pan and add the rest of the butter and cook the other half.

Toast the bread and butter well. Divide the roes between the bread and serve with lemon wedges.

INDIVIDUAL YORKSHIRE PUDDINGS WITH GOLDEN SYRUP

The Yorkshire pudding batter can be done the night before so you are ready to go in the morning. This is a very substantial breakfast, not very healthy, but delicious. To ease the guilt, I suggest a good walk afterwards.

Serves 6

100g plain flour
Salt
3 medium eggs
200ml full fat milk
50ml dripping or sunflower oil
6 large tbsp golden syrup

First mix the flour and salt in a large bowl. Make a well in the centre, add the eggs and mix well. Gradually add the milk, beat until smooth, cover and allow to rest for 1 hour.

Put the oil into 6 individual Yorkshire pudding tins and put into the oven at 220°C and make sure it is sizzling hot before you pour the batter in. Put into the oven and cook for 15 minutes approx. Remove and serve with a good drizzle of golden syrup on top.

TOAD IN THE HOLE WITH VENISON SAUSAGES

You can buy some very good venison sausages today, but I thought I would include a recipe in case you feel you would like to make them yourself. This will make more than 8 sausages, but you can freeze whatever is left over.

Serves 4-6

For the sausages
500g venison shoulder, finely minced
300g belly of pork, minced
25g parsley, finely chopped
Salt and pepper
25g stale breadcrumbs
1 tsp juniper, finely chopped
Sausage casings
25g lard

For the Yorkshire pudding
200g plain flour
Pinch of salt
4 eggs
400ml full fat milk
50g duck fat or sunflower oil

Put the venison mince, pork mince, parsley, salt, pepper, breadcrumbs and juniper berries into a large bowl and mix well. To test for the seasoning, fry a small patty in pan with a drizzle of oil. Once cooked, taste and if needed add more salt and pepper to the mixture.

Put the sausage meat into the casings. This really needs to be done with a sausage machine. Allow to rest for at least an hour before you fry; overnight would be even better. Melt the lard in a pan and fry 8 sausages on a medium heat until they are browned all over.

For the Yorkshire pudding, mix the flour and salt in a large bowl. Add the egg and beat well as you add the milk, continue beating until smooth. Allow to rest for 1 hour.

Add the chopped thyme to the batter and season well. Heat the duck fat in a roasting tin until sizzling. Put the browned sausages in the tin and cover with the batter. Bake in the oven at 220°C for 20 to 25 minutes until well risen and golden. Remove from the tin and serve.

FISH AND CHIPS WITH MUSHY PEAS

Mushy peas are made with marrowfat peas, which need to be soaked overnight. They are a traditional northern English accompaniment to fish and I make my mine richer by adding butter. It all means that this is a very substantial breakfast, but one which just occasionally is irresistible.

Serves 4

For the peas
200g dried marrowfat peas
2 level tsp bicarbonate of soda
40g butter
Cayenne pepper
1 tsp sugar
Salt and white pepper

For the fish
200g self-raising flour
110g corn flour
100ml milk
300ml sparkling water
Salt and white pepper
4 haddock fillets, skinned and pin bones removed, 180g each
Salt and pepper
100g plain flour

For the chips
1kg Maris Piper potatoes, peeled and cut into batons
Sunflower oil for deep fat frying

First put the peas into water and soak overnight. Drain well then place in a large saucepan with 700ml of water. Cover and cook for 30 to 40 minutes until very soft and mushy. Add the butter, sugar, cayenne pepper and season. Mix well and these will now be ready to serve.

To make the batter for the fish, combine the two flours and gradually add the milk and then the water, whisking well until no lumps are left. Season with salt and white pepper.

To cook the fish, dredge the fillets in the plain flour and shake off any excess. Dip into the batter then fry in sunflower oil at 180°C for approx 6 minutes, making sure they are golden all over.

Put the potato batons into the oil at 150°C for 10 minutes, then increase the heat to 180°C for a further 5 to 8 minutes cooking. Remove, drain and season with salt before serving.

CHAPTER 7

BREADS AND BAKING

If you have time there is nothing nicer than freshly baked bread. You can make a large batch then put it in the freezer. I always think it is worth it and it also gives you the opportunity to control the salt quantity. I always think it is worth spending a few pennies more on good organic flour from a local miller. I use Sunflour which is only down the road from where I live and if you can, use fresh yeast - your local baker or the bread department of many supermarkets will most likely have some.

WHOLEMEAL LOAF

I have added some white flour to this wholemeal bread because I like a lighter loaf. But if you want to have a dense loaf, use all wholemeal.

350g wholemeal flour
350g strong white flour
20g fresh yeast or 7g dried yeast
475ml tepid water
10g fine salt

Put both the flours in a large bowl and crumble in the yeast. Add the water to form a dough and then place onto a lightly floured surface. Put your hands into a bowl of flour and shake off any excess, now start to stretch the dough with the palm of your hand, then roll back, turn a quarter turn and stretch again. Continue doing this for about 7 minutes.

Now add the salt, which will draw the water out and allow the dough to soften again. Continue stretching for a further 7 minutes or until there is a good elasticity. Make the dough into a round and place into a floured bowl. Cover with cling wrap and leave for about 1½ hours or until it has doubled in volume.

To knock back, remove the risen dough and knead for 30 seconds. Place into a 900g buttered bread tin and allow to rise again for a further 45 minutes or until it has doubled in size again.

Place in pre-heated oven at 220°C for 25 minutes. Turn the heat down to 150°C and cook for a further 20 minutes.

Remove from the oven and put onto a rack and allow to cool. If the bottom needs to be crisped up put back into the oven upside down for a further 7 minutes and then again allow to cool before cutting, otherwise it will be too doughy.

SODA BREAD

I always think it is so useful having an instant bread that you can just churn out. This is it. Keith Hemming, a baker from Ireland, showed me how to make the perfect soda bread. The important thing to remember is not to overwork the dough otherwise it can become too heavy.

500g plain flour
1 tsp salt
2½ tsp bicarbonate of soda
1 dstsp sunflower oil
500ml buttermilk

Put the plain flour into a large bowl, add the salt and bicarbonate of soda, mix well. Now add the oil and the buttermilk. Carefully bring everything together, keeping the dough as light as possible. Make into a round and place onto a floured tray. Score a cross on the top and sprinkle with flour. Place in a preheated oven at 220°C for 20 minutes. Turn down to 150°C and cook for a further 25 minutes. If the knock on the bottom sounds hollow it's done, if the sound is flat put back in the oven upside down for a further 5 minutes. Remove and place onto a rack to cool.

FARMHOUSE LOAF

A wonderful homemade crusty farmhouse loaf is one of the most delicious breads for breakfast.

650g white flour strong
15g fresh yeast or 7g dried yeast
450ml water tepid
10g salt

Put the flour into a bowl with the fresh yeast. Make sure it's all crumbled in well. Add the water to form a dough and then place onto a lightly floured surface. Put your hands into a bowl of flour and shake off any excess, now start to stretch the dough with the palm of your hand, then roll back, turn a quarter turn and stretch again. Continue doing this for about 7 minutes.

Now add the salt, which will draw the water out and allow the dough to soften again. Continue stretching for a further 7 minutes or until there is a good elasticity. Make the dough into a round and place into a floured bowl. Cover with cling wrap and leave for about 1 hour or until it has doubled in volume.

To knock back, remove the risen dough from the bowl and knead for 30 seconds. Place into a buttered 900g bread tin and make 8 incisions along the loaf diagonally. Allow to rise again for a further 30 minutes or until it doubles in size again. Sprinkle with flour.

Place in a preheated oven at 220°C for 30 minutes. Turn the heat down to 150°C and cook for a further 15 minutes. Remove from the oven and turn out. I sometimes put the loaf back in the oven if the bottom needs a little longer, for a further 7 minutes approx.

Allow to cool before cutting, otherwise it will be too doughy.

SEEDED LOAF

This is a great healthy alternative to a normal loaf and I love all the seeds which run through it. Sunflour makes flour which is already mixed with seeds, but you can make it yourself from scratch.

400g whole wheat stone ground flour

200g white strong flour

20g fresh yeast or 7g dried yeast

450ml tepid water

30g honey, runny

15g linseed (flax seed)

15g poppy seeds

25g sesame seeds

25g sunflower seeds

25g oat bran

10g salt

1 tbsp extra mixed seeds to sprinkle on top

Put the flour into a large bowl and crumble in the fresh yeast. Add the water, honey, seeds and bran, and mix together to make into a dough. Place onto a lightly floured surface. Start by stretching the dough with the palm of your hand, then roll back, turn a quarter turn, then stretch again. Continue doing this for about 7 minutes. If it gets too sticky dust your hands in a little flour, but be sure to remove any excess by clapping your hands together. Now add the salt, which will draw the water out and allow the dough to soften again. Continue stretching for a further 7 minutes or until there is a good elasticity.

Make the dough into a round and put into a floured bowl. Cover with cling wrap and allow to rise for 1 hour or until double in volume. To knock back, remove the risen dough from the bowl and knead for 30 seconds. Place into 2 small oiled loaf tins and put somewhere warm and allow to rise uncovered for 1 hour approximately. Wet the tops of the loaves and sprinkle with seeds. Put into a preheated oven at 220°C for 25 minutes. Turn down to 150°C and bake for a further 20 minutes.

It is delicious toasted and served with a spoonful of cream cheese, a few slices of cucumber and lots of black pepper.

ENGLISH MUFFINS

These soft muffins don't require strong flour and they aren't worked like ordinary bread. This is a sticky dough, so you will need to keep your hands well floured. Simply put your hands into a bowl of flour, then clap off the excess, which will prevent over-flouring of the dough and help keep it light.

Makes 10 approx.

250ml tepid water
200ml milk
15g fresh yeast or 4g dried yeast
700g plain flour
10g salt
1 large egg, whisked

First heat the water and milk to blood heat. Crumble in the fresh yeast and whisk well until it has melted. Leave for 10 minutes to start fermenting.

In a large bowl put in the plain flour with the salt and add the egg. When ready, add the milk yeast mixture. Mix and knead gently. It will be sticky, but keep your hands well floured. Now put into a floured bowl and allow to rise for 1 hour or until it has doubled in volume. Remove from the bowl and place on a floured surface. Knock back and roll out to 1cm thick and leave for a further 15 minutes. Cut into 8cm rounds. Place the dough on a floured baking tray. Put into the oven at 220°C for 12 to 15 minutes approx until golden brown.

PIKELETS

Pikelets are so very Yorkshire. They are absolutely delicious with strawberry jam and while they are normally eaten at tea-time, I love them for breakfast.

Serves 8

200g self-raising flour
1 rounded tsp bicarbonate of soda
3 tbsp caster sugar
Pinch of salt
350ml milk
1 whole egg
1 egg yolk
100g butter

Put the flour into a large bowl and add the bicarbonate of soda, caster sugar, salt and mix well. Add the milk, egg and egg yolk to the flour. Mix and whisk well, removing any lumps.

In a non-stick pan add a little of the butter and heat on a medium heat. Spoon in three tablespoons of the mixture, cook slowly until it starts to bubble, then turn over. You must try to keep the heat down because you don't want to burn them.

Keep warm and repeat until all the mixture has been used.

BANANA BREAD

I really put this in for fun. I have a friend who eats a banana sandwich for breakfast every morning, so Peter this is an alternative way to have your banana!

80g butter
160g unrefined golden caster sugar
2 eggs, beaten
450g ripe bananas
250g self-raising flour
½ tsp salt
½ tsp bicarbonate of soda

In a mixing bowl, beat the butter and sugar until very soft. Add the eggs and beat again. Mash the bananas and add to the mixture. Now sieve in the flour, salt and bicarbonate of soda. Mix well. Put into a greased and floured 700g loaf tin and place into the oven at 180°C for 1 hour approx (test with a skewer to see that it comes out clean). Remove from the tin and put onto a rack to cool.

BRIOCHE LOAF OR BUNS

Brioche is such good bread to make; it rises in the fridge so you can prepare it the night before. It's a bread for special occasions so just don't think of the calories. If you do not have a dough hook, the method can be done by hand. However, this is one occasion where I do not advise it as you will find the mixture far too sticky.

Extra butter for greasing

500g strong white flour

40g fresh yeast or
14g dried yeast

30g sugar

10g salt

6 whole eggs

225g unsalted butter,
very soft

Egg to glaze

1 large 900g loaf tin or 2 small brioche tins.

Butter the loaf tin or mini brioche tins. In a large mixing bowl put in the flour, then crumble in the fresh yeast, add the sugar and salt, mix well. Now add the eggs one by one, mixing all the time (this is good to do with a dough hook). Beat for at least 5 minutes, now add the very soft butter bit by bit, do not add too quickly otherwise it could become a cake batter. Make sure each time you add the butter it is well incorporated. This will take up to 10 minutes, but patience is a virtue in this case. Keep beating for a further 5 minutes, so it's lovely, shiny and slides off the dough hook.

Remove the dough from the bowl, put onto a lightly floured surface and shape, then put into the loaf tin, or make small balls and put into the medium brioche tins for the baby brioche.

Put into the fridge overnight then remove in the morning. Brush the tops with egg and put the loaf in the oven for 25 minutes at 220°C then for 20 to 25 minutes at 140°C. For the small brioche, put into the oven at 220°C for 15 minutes approx.

OATCAKES

When I was working in Scotland I absolutely adored oatcakes for breakfast. The traditional Yorkshire ones are made with yeast and are cooked on one side only on top of a griddle, but I find this variation a lot easier to make.

Makes 20–25

125g butter
350g medium oatmeal
100g flour plain
25g oatbran
1 level tsp bicarbonate of soda
1 tsp salt
1 tsp sugar
3 tbsp water

Place 2 flat trays in the oven at 180°C.

Put the butter, together with all the dry ingredients, into a food processor and make into breadcrumbs. This can be done in a bowl with your fingertips, but it just takes a little longer. Now add 2 tbsp of water and bring together into a pliable but stiff dough. Lightly flour a surface and carefully roll out the oatmeal. Be careful because it cracks easily. With an ordinary cutlery knife cut into 20 to 25 squares, depending how big you want them. Place the oatcakes onto the preheated trays and put in the oven for 20 minutes at 180°C. Remove when they are pale golden brown.

FRUIT AND SEED FLAPJACK

A traditional flapjack contains just four ingredients, but adding some fruit makes them much more interesting.

Makes 20-24

100g golden syrup
35g brown sugar
200g unsalted butter
350g porridge oats

25g dried apricots, finely chopped
25g dried figs, finely chopped
25g dried cranberries
25g sunflower seeds
25g pumpkin seeds

Grease a 23cm x 30cm baking tin, line with baking paper and grease again. Put the golden syrup, brown sugar and butter in a saucepan and melt until everything is well dissolved. Add the porridge oats and mix well. Add the fruit and seeds and mix well again. Put into the lined tin, spread well and press down with the back of a spoon. Put into preheated oven at 170°C for 20 to 25 minutes, remove and cut into 20-24 flapjacks.

• You can also use flax seeds, chopped almonds, raisins or sultanas.

CHAPTER 8

JAMS AND PRESERVES

Jams and preserves are a great way to use fruit when they are in abundance and my friend Elsbeth who runs Rosebud Preserves has spent a long time perfecting her wonderful jams, jellies and chutneys. When I was doing a show in New York the home economist said he had some wonderful jelly for me and proudly showed me a jar Rosebud Preserves. When I told him it was made in a village a couple of miles away from my home he was very surprised and just a little disappointed that I already knew of their wonderful jams. If you have the time, however, it is worth having a go at making your own.

There is nothing better than homemade marmalade or jams. It's a wonderful way of preserving the fruit at the height of the season for all those wonderful long weekend breakfasts throughout the year. The most important rule is the fruit must be fresh and firm. It's also better to have it slightly under ripe rather than over ripe.

You will need a large wide saucepan. I find it must never be more than half-full, to ensure the fruit does not boil over. I also find preserving or granulating sugars are the best and I sometimes use extra pectin if the fruit is low in pectin, to help with the setting. Temperature is all important in jam making, so the one thing that does help is a sugar thermometer. If you need to thicken the jam, just keep boiling, testing the consistency every 15 minutes.

To sterilise the bottles, first wash well then pour boiling water into them. Put the jam into warm jars, put wax paper round on top then place the lids on and screw tightly while the jam is still warm. If you don't have lids use cellophane.

RASPBERRY JAM

2kg raspberries
Juice of 1
lemon, strained
800g
granulated or
preserving sugar

First remove any stalks and hull the raspberries. Put them into a large wide saucepan. Bring to a simmer and cook gently for 5-6 minutes until the fruit is soft, keep stirring occasionally, now add the sugar and lemon, stir well. Bring slowly to the boil, and keep soft boiling until it reaches setting point, skimming the top of the jam as you go. This could take 20 to 25 minutes. Now put into warm jam jars and put a wax paper round on top then put on a lid if available and screw tightly. If you have no lids put on cellophane. To test whether the jam is done the temperature should be between 104°C to 107°C. I put a spoonful of the jam onto a cold plate I've had in the freezer. If it ripples it should be set, but if not simmer for a little longer.

STRAWBERRY JAM

I always make plenty of this strawberry jam when it is in season. I have used 250g hulled strawberries in this recipe so you will need to start off with a few more than that quantity. It is worth the effort hulling them properly.

2.5kg hulled strawberries
Juice of 3 lemons, strained
1.5kg granulated sugar

To remove the stalks and core from the strawberries you take a small pairing knife and just cut around into the strawberry and the white core will come out. Wash the strawberries under cold water and put them into a very large pan. This is important because of the bubbling boiling syrup, so it can come up without going over the top. Put on to a medium heat and bring up slowly to a simmer, this will take a few minutes. Once simmering cook for 8 – 10 minutes, now add the sugar and stir and cook for a further 10 minutes, now add the lemon juice and cook for approximately 25 – 30 minutes or until it reaches setting point, skimming the top of the jam as you go. I put from between 104°C – 107°C. I put a spoonful of jam on a very cold plate and if it ripples it should be set. If not simmer for a little longer.

PEAR AND GINGER JAM

3cm piece of fresh ginger, finely chopped

2kg pears, peeled, cored and cut into ½ cm dice

Rind and juice of 2 lemons

500ml water approximately

1kg sugar approximately

5 pieces stem ginger, finely chopped

You will need a piece of clean muslin cloth. Into this put the fresh ginger with the rind and the pips of the lemon. Tie up with string. Put the pears and juice of the lemon into a saucepan with the water and the bag of muslin and bring up slowly to heat and simmer for 15 to 20 minutes approximately or until the pears are soft. Now add the sugar and stem ginger to the pears and cook for a further 50-60 minutes or until it's at setting point, skimming the top of the jam as you go. It is important to stir occasionally so it doesn't catch on the bottom. Now when it is done squeeze as much out of the muslin as possible to gain all the lovely ginger flavour.

To test whether the jam is done the temperature should be between 104°C to 107°C. I put a spoonful of the jam onto a cold plate I've had in the freezer. If it ripples it should be set, but if not simmer for a little longer. When it is done put into sterilised jars. You should have around 2kgs in weight.

LEMON CURD

As it can be made at any time of the year, this recipe makes only a small quantity of lemon curd. If you want to double the quantity, go ahead, just remember it will take longer to thicken.

Makes 3 jars approx
180g unsalted butter
400g caster sugar
4 eggs
Zest and juice of 4 lemons
1 tsp corn flour

Put all the ingredients into a bowl over a pan of boiling water, making sure the bottom of the bowl is not touching the water. Whisk until everything has melted. Remove from the heat and put the mixture through a sieve. Rinse the bowl and whisk. Return the curd to the bowl, place back over the pan of boiling water and continue stirring. Cook until the mixture thickens, which can take up to 40 minutes. Pour into sterilised warm jars and allow to cool before sealing.

MARGARITA'S SEVILLE MARMALADE

A Yorkshire lady called Margarita gave me this recipe and it is just delicious.

Makes 4kgs.

1.35kg Seville oranges
2 lemons
2.7kg sugar
1 dstsp black treacle
3 litres water

Simmer the fruit whole in the water on a low heat for 1 ½ hours. Remove the fruit but leave the pan on the heat. Cut open the fruit, add the pips to the water and reduce to liquid to 1 litre in volume. Strain to remove the pips. Remove the flesh and pith from the oranges and cut the peel into strips. Add to the reduced liquid with the sugar and the treacle and boil to 104°C–107°C or until set. Pour into warm sterilised jars.

DAMSON CHEESE

Sometimes I really enjoy just a piece of cheese or meat for breakfast the continental style, but I like to have some sweetness to go with it. Damson cheese, which is not a dairy product, but a thick preserve, is perfect. This is so good to have with a strong cheddar or just on scones.

1.5kg damsons, washed
1 tbsp crushed juniper
1 lemon peel
200ml water
1.5kg granulated sugar

Put the damsons, crushed juniper and lemon peel into a saucepan with the water. Bring to the boil then turn the heat down and simmer gently for 8 to 10 minutes or until the fruit is very soft. Put the fruit through a fine sieve. Allowing equal quantities of sugar to damson pulp, put into a pan and cook until it becomes a very thick consistency. Put into sterilised jars. Pour into the sterilised warm jars and allow to cool before sealing.

CHAPTER 8

DRINKS

Smoothies are a quick and convenient way to start the day. Anything goes in terms of taste. You can also add bran or wheat germ or oats and have an all in one breakfast in a drink. Or you can get the children to come up with their own recipes. It is a wonderful way of getting them to eat some of their five a day. I also love fresh mint tea. I enjoy in the summer going out and picking my mint in the morning.

ICED TEA

I first drank this in the South of France, it's the most thirst quenching drink I know and if you like, add a bit of fresh mint.

Makes 2 litres

5 teabags
2 litres boiling water
10 sugar lumps
2 lemons

Put the teabags and sugar into a medium teapot with boiling water. Allow to get cold. In a 2 litre jug add the tea topped up with water to the top. Slice and add the lemons and put into the fridge to get very cold.

ICED COFFEE

Serves 1

125 ml freshly made strong black coffee (allow to cool and then chill)
150ml full fat milk, chilled
3 ice cubes, or more if required
2 tsp sugar or to taste

First put the chilled fresh coffee and milk and the sugar into a liquidiser with the ice. Whiz up until very smooth. Put into a tall glass and serve.

FRESH MINT TEA

There is nothing more refreshing than a cup of fresh mint tea and it is so easy and cheap to make. I love going to pick the mint in the morning and I always have a ceramic pot outside the back door growing.

Serves 2

Handful of fresh mint
Boiling water

Put the mint into a warmed teapot then add the boiling water and allow to infuse for 2 minutes.

HOT CHOCOLATE WITH CINNAMON AND CREAM

Serves 2

1 rounded tsp cocoa powder
275 ml full fat milk
2 tsp sugar to taste
Pinch of cinnamon to taste, optional
2 tsp whipped cream

Put a rounded teaspoon of cocoa powder into a mug. Boil the milk, add a little to the cocoa to make a paste. Add the sugar and cinnamon and top up with the rest of the milk, stirring well, then finish with a teaspoon of lightly whipped cream.

FRESH ORANGE JUICE

Serves 2

4 oranges

I always squeeze 2 oranges per person. There is nothing nicer than freshly squeezed orange or grapefruit juice. I tend to go for thin skinned oranges rather than the thick skinned ones.

BANANA AND BLUEBERRY SMOOTHIE

Makes 2 large glasses

½ banana
200g blueberries
200ml natural yoghurt

1 tbsp oat bran
A large handful of ice
1 tsp runny honey
Juice of 1 lemon
100 ml milk

Put everything into a liquidiser and purée until smooth. Serve.

MANGO AND BANANA SMOOTHIE

Makes 2 large glasses

1 ripe mango, skinned and pip removed
½ banana

Juice of 1 lime
200ml plain yoghurt
100ml milk
A large handful of ice

Put everything into a liquidiser and purée until smooth. Serve.

STRAWBERRY SMOOTHIE

Makes 2 large glasses

250g strawberries
200ml natural yoghurt

100ml milk
Juice of 1 orange
1 tbsp caster sugar
A large handful of ice

Put everything into a liquidiser and purée until smooth. Serve.

BUCK'S FIZZ

I always love a celebration breakfast and it's not complete without the Buck's Fizz.

Serves 4

8 oranges or a carton of fresh orange juice
4 small strawberries (optional)
1 bottle
Champagne

First squeeze the oranges, strain the juice and put it into a jug and place in the fridge to get very cold. I use one part orange juice to two parts Champagne. The trick is to pour the orange juice in first, add a small strawberry and then top with Champagne.

BLOODY MARY

To have a Virgin Mary, just leave out the vodka.

Serves 1
Ice
Vodka, double shot
150ml tomato juice
½ tsp Worcestershire sauce
½ tsp horseradish sauce
A dash of Tabasco
Pepper
Celery stick

Put the ice into a long glass with the vodka, then add the tomato juice and all the other ingredients. Mix well and serve with a celery stick.

CONVERSION CHARTS

TEMPERATURES

140°C	275°F	Gas mark 1	200°C	400°F	Gas mark 6
150°C	300°F	Gas mark 2	220°C	425°F	Gas mark 7
170°C	325°F	Gas mark 3	230°C	450°F	Gas mark 8
180°C	350°F	Gas mark 4	240°C	475°F	Gas mark 9
190°C	375°F	Gas mark 5	250°C	500°F	Gas mark 10

SOLIDS

25g	=	1oz
50g	=	2oz
75g	=	3oz
110g	=	4oz
125g	=	4.5oz
150g	=	5oz
175g	=	6oz
225g	=	8oz
250g	=	9oz
325g	=	12oz
350g	=	12.5oz
375g	=	13oz
400g	=	14oz
450g	=	1lb
700g	=	1.5lbs
1.1kg	=	2.5lbs

LIQUIDS

25ml	=	1fl oz
50ml	=	2f oz
75ml	=	3fl oz
100ml	=	4 fl oz
125ml	=	4.5fl oz
150ml	=	5fl oz
175ml	=	6fl oz
200ml	=	7fl oz
225ml	=	8fl oz
250ml	=	8.5fl oz
275ml	=	½pt
300ml	=	10.5fl oz
350ml	=	12fl oz
400ml	=	14fl oz
450ml	=	16fl oz
575ml	=	1pt

STOCKISTS

Where I live, I'm lucky to be blessed with some great producers. When it comes to breakfast, the sausages come from Beavers, the bacon I like to use is Anna's Happy Trotters and the black pudding is either from the Blue Pig Company or Arthur Haigh. I've listed here some of my favourite shops and producers. Many of them now do online deliveries, but really it's just a question of getting out there and seeing what's on your own doorstep.

ANNA'S HAPPY TROTTERS

Burland
Holme Road
Howden
East Yorkshire
DN14 7LY
Contact: 01430 433030
www.annashappytrotters.com

BLUE PIG COMPANY

Mearbeck
Long Preston
Skipton
North Yorkshire
BD23 4QP
Contact: 07939 117366
www.bluepigcompany.com

BEAVERS BUTCHER

11 Silver Street
Masham
North Yorkshire
HG4 4DX
Contact: 01765 689269

CARRICKS (FISH) LTD

Yew Tree House
Snape
Bedale
North Yorkshire
DL8 2TJ
Contact: 01677 470261
www.carrickfishltd.co.uk

FORTUNE'S KIPPERS

Henrietta Street
Whitby
North Yorkshire
YO22 4PW
Contact: 01947 601659
www.fortuneskippers.co.uk

ROSEBUDS PRESERVES

Rosebud Farm
Healey, nr Masham
North Yorkshire
HG4 4LH
Contact: 01765 689174
www.rosebudpreserves.co.uk

STEENBERGS ORGANIC

6 Hallikeld Close
Barker Business Park
Melmerby
Ripon
North Yorkshire
HG4 5GZ
Contact: 01765 640088
www.steenbergs.co.uk

SUNFLOURS

The Hutts Mill
Grewelthorpe
Ripon
North Yorkshire
HG4 3DA
Contact: 01765 658534
www.sunflours.com

SWINTON TROUT FARM

Sawmill Cottage
Healey, nr Masham
North Yorkshire
HG4 4LB
Contact: 01765 689270

YORKSHIRE DALES CHEESE COMPANY

Lowlands
Low Street
Leeming Bar, Northallerton
North Yorkshire
DL7 9BN
Contact: 01677 423248
www.yorkshiredalescheese.co.uk

WENSLEYDALE CREAMERY

Gayle Lane
Hawes
Wensleydale
North Yorkshire
DL8 3RN
Contact: 01969 667664
www.wensleydale.co.uk

Arthur Haigh supply a number of shops in Yorkshire and also have an online ordering facility. For more details visit www.yorkshireblackpudding.co.uk or call 01845 578227.

INDEX

ACKNOWLEDGEMENTS

It may be my name on the front of this book, but it would not have been possible without the hard work of so many people. So thank you to Belinda Bemrose my wonderful PA, who has the unenviable job of deciphering my ghastly writing, for her enduring patience. Thank you to Heather Holden-Brown, my wonderful literary agent, for all her unwavering support and also to the lovely Elly James in her office. Thank you to Sue Hiscoe for her amazing photographs and the time she put into making this a wonderful book. Thank you to Gilly Robinson for her patience and support in interpreting the recipes just how I like them. Also thank you to David Burrill for listening and guiding me in making this a team effort. Thank you to Sarah Freeman for great planning and putting in many unsociable hours. Thank you to Roger Arnold for his great crab salad and fun days on location. Also thank you to Barry Cox and Patricia Lennon for all their support. I would also like to thank all my wonderful suppliers for their great produce: Anna's Happy Trotters, Arthur Haigh, Beavers Butcher, Blue Pig Company, Carricks (Fish) Ltd , Fortune's Kippers, W.S Rogers & Sons (butchers), Rosebuds Preserves, Steenbergs Organic, Sunflours, Swinton Trout Farm, Yorkshire Dales Cheese Company and Wensleydale Creamery. Also a huge thank you to all at Swinton Hall. And of course, thank you to my family for always being there.

Also available from Great Northern Books:

EDGE OF HEAVEN
THE YORKSHIRE COAST
Personal Reflections from our Finest writers
Featuring contributions from:
Ian Clayton | Margaret Drabble | R.J. Ellory | Lee Hanson
Roy Hattersley | David Joy | Ian McMillan | W.R. Mitchell
Blake Morrison | Alan Plater | Selina Scott | Martin Wainwright

THE GREAT BOOK OF RHUBARB
by Elaine Lemm

THE GREAT BOOK OF YORKSHIRE PUDDING
by Elaine Lemm

BRONTË IN LOVE
The most tragic story Charlotte never told was her own
By Sarah Freeman

Visit www.greatnorthernbooks.co.uk